The Rainbow Earth

Also by Don C. Nix

Loss of Being
The Field of Being
Moments of Grace
Patterns of Being
Dancing with Presence
The Crucible of the Miraculous
The Matrix of Splendor

The Rainbow Earth

Expanding Consciousness and Perception

Don C. Nix, J.D., Ph.D.

iUniverse, Inc.
New York   Bloomington

iUniverse books may be ordered through booksellers or by contacting:

iUniverse
1663 Liberty Drive
Bloomington, IN 47403
www.iuniverse.com
1-800-Authors (1-800-288-4677)

Because of the dynamic nature of the Internet, any Web addresses or links contained in this book may have changed since publication and may no longer be valid. The views expressed in this work are solely those of the author and do not necessarily reflect the views of the publisher, and the publisher hereby disclaims any responsibility for them.

ISBN: 978-1-4502-6232-3 (sc)
ISBN: 978-1-4502-6233-0 (ebook)

Printed in the United States of America

iUniverse rev. date: 10/1/2010

Dedication

To my grandmother, Georgia Rice, now long vanished, who took a moment to tenderly touch my hair and face and look searchingly into my eyes to see who was there. I still remember this moment 65 years later.

Don C. Nix
Sonoma, California
September 2010

Contents

Dedication   1

Introduction   5

1   Rainbows all around us   6

2   The Garden is within us   7

3   The world is always fresh   8

4   We stand on the shores of Immensity   9

5   Have you ever cut your finger   10

6   I'm spinning on the earth   11

7   Life has its highs and lows   12

8   Something fills my heart with joy   13

9   Feel the potential in the air   14

10 There are dark spots in my soul   15

11 We are swimming   16

12 Our general arc is upward   17

13 Raise your head and celebrate   18

14 I take the bow of my mind   19

15 How can I draw myself   20

16 Sophistication is the enemy   21

17 The Cosmos is dancing   22

18 I'm looking for the metaphor   23

19 Moment by moment   24

20 The well is deep   25

21 Loveliness is all around us   26

22 We're moving toward the Formless Realm   27

23 Open your eyes to wonder   28

24 I am patiently waiting   29

25 Give me a moment of Your time   30

26 I cannot see why I'm here   31

27 This is the first moment   32

28 A titan of industry   33

29 I am a confluence of forces   34

30 Have I been all that I could be   35

31 The world is arising   36

32 Something is holding the world together   37

33 I know that I'm a primate   38

34 I'm surrounded by chimera   39

35 The Buddhists call it mindfulness   40

36 This is the feeling   41

37 You cannot die into emptiness   42

38 We are living in a rainbow world   43

39 Something moves me through my day   44

40 I want to dig deeper into myself   45

41 If I was the only person on Earth   46

42 I want to put myself in contact   47

43 Do you believe in destiny   48

44 I'm trying to grow myself bigger   49

45 The earth spins effortlessly   50

46 I wait for the touch   51

47 I bow my head   52

48 We cannot understand our life   53

49 Open my eyes   54

50 How should we hold them in our heart   55

51 There's more to me   56

52 We are a moving stream   57

53 Apes on the earth   58

54 We might yet be saved   59

55 So many memories   60

56 How should we view   61

57 If I could go deeper   62

58 My subject is eternity   63

59 I know that You are everything   64

60 How do I align myself   65

61 Waiting for understanding   66

62 Make a comrade of loss   67

63 Who is in charge here   68

64 Morning arrives with its radiance   69

65 What if we are not the doer   70

66 If I clear my mind   71

67 It's a great gift to be human   72

68 I bow to the moon   73

69 What are we becoming   74

70 Somewhere galaxies are colliding   75

71 Under the clamor of the world   76

72 Creativity is a flow   77

73 We march side by side with others   78

74 When you're nearing the end of the road   79

75 Can you grasp how precious your life is   80

76 Something that is greater than me   81

77 You cannot be overlooked   82

Introduction

We see only a fraction of what is around us. This is both a literal and a figurative truth. Scientists tell us that if the full spectrum of light was the height of a skyscraper, the part that our eyes can see would be less than 10 feet of that building. In the same way, we are so preoccupied with our internal conversation with ourselves, and with our passing problems, that we miss most of Reality. We are conditioned creatures. We learn early to screen out much of Life. As we grow, we progressively lose our access to freshness and newness. Our perception narrows and atrophies, and we begin to live in a grey, rather uninteresting world. We have learned to miss most of Reality.

At moments these veils can lift, and we can be stunned by the beauty and harmony around us. The simplest things can move us to wonder. Psychologists have called these peak experiences, but they could be our normal state of perception. How can we wake up, get past our conceptual veils, and directly experience the world, life, ourselves, other people and the Cosmos? A strong beginning would be to see the universe as living, intelligent, conscious, creative and unfolding. In short, to re-integrate Being into our world-view.

The 77 poems in this little book are all about the struggle to develop this new awareness. It takes time and some dedication to build a new worldview, but the rewards are immense. The miraculous Cosmos is presenting Itself for our wondrous inspection in every moment. We only need to wake up and learn to see.

1

Rainbows all around us.
Brilliancy sparkles here.
We are living inside a diamond
that reflects the colored light.
We are walking through the Cosmos
thinking,
breathing,
receiving,
perceiving,
living out the arc of our lives,
creating our own sweet narrative,
powered by Vastness beyond our sight.

2

The Garden is within us,
full of luscious fruits,
and clear, cool water,
and moments of ecstasy.
But, fixated on the siren world
we look outward,
searching,
searching,
searching,
for the thing that will
bring true delight.
We're looking in the wrong place.
This is the way it's always been.
While we scan the world
for what we need,
the delights are all within.

3

The world is always fresh,
newly minted,
arising from the depths of Being,
with the residue
of the morning dew
still invisibly upon it.
The world is recreated,
moment to moment,
from the limitless well
of Potential,
appearing in its perfection,
perfectly conceived,
perfectly collated,
perfectly harmonious,
sublime in its artless beauty
crafted over eons,
and presented now
to our astonished eyes.
It is always morning somewhere.

4

We stand on the shores of Immensity,
looking skyward and reaching up,
struggling to understand our role
but not truly able to see.
In a Cosmos of black and silence
we're trying to see past the veils.
We cower before the Boundless
and are fixated on details.
What if we blew through our limits?
What if we opened our eyes?
What if we suddenly took our place
in this Cosmos of Living Space?

5

Have you ever cut your finger
and watched it heal itself?
Did you know you were watching miracle
unfold before your eyes?
What Force orchestrated this healing
and carried it to fruition?
What Mind brought all together
this group of talented cells?
What Power conceived this process
and passed it in DNA,
so that you could continue living
in a restored way today?

6

I'm spinning on the earth
as I sit in my chair,
dreaming and musing
and trying to see
before the break of day.
The stars are spinning too
in the darkened night-time sky,
dancing and promenading
as is their ancient way.
I know that I am transient.
I'm only passing through.
But, blessed as I am with consciousness,
I can see the Cosmic view.

7

Life has its highs and lows.
We are tumbled around
and burned and hit
in a process that's rough and harsh.
We long for a measure of safety.
We long to be sheltered from harm,
but we're in the wrong Cosmos for that.
Safety is not our destiny.
We must take our licks
and the blows and kicks,
and keep on marching resolutely.
We are part of Something vast,
and mysterious and obscure.
We cannot perceive why we're here,
but we know that somehow we have a role.
We must play it in spite of our fear.

8

Something fills my heart with joy.
Something fires my nerves with bliss.
Something is moving me through my life,
and expanding me,
and making me see.
A fire has been lit within my soul.
It's burning fiercely now.
It lifts me out of the trivial me
and directs my gaze
to the Cosmic Sea.

9

Feel the potential in the air.
The Cosmos is yearning to bloom.
Life is unfolding
and showing Itself
and leading us God knows where.
We are spectators on this journey.
Our trip is conducted by Other.
We're along for the ride.
Hold onto your hat,
as Life pushes Itself ever further.

10

There are dark spots in my soul,
places of contraction
that hinder my unfolding.
I sense them there inside me,
but I cannot see their shape.
Sometimes they rise
to my conscious mind
and I understand their place.
I see where they came from,
and why they formed,
and how I might best dissolve them.
I need to move through them now.
I need to move out of their grip,
if the Force of Life
is ever to rush,
unimpeded,
through the riverbed of my being.

11

We are swimming
in a Sea of consciousness,
The Cosmos is awake and aware.
The Sea is laced with meaning,
full of joy and not despair.
Life is efflorescing.
Maturity is coming.
Though we all feel quite impatient,
it will take a while
to get us there.
We are works in progress,
changing,
evolving,
developing,
and going we know not where.
Relax.
It's a marathon, not a sprint.

12

Our general arc is upward.
In a turbulent world
it's hard to see
where we're going
or how we'll get there.
The Cosmos is unfolding us.
It takes Its own sweet time.
Its plan is hidden from our gaze.
It does not lack invention.
We're pummeled and tumbled
and crushed and whirled
as we're molded by Its intention.
It's much too early to despair.
We must take a longer view.
We're not yet a finished product.
We're metamorphosing moment to moment,
as the World builds Itself
with cunning and with care.

13

Raise your head and celebrate!
You have been plucked
from nothingness
to walk the earth,
to grow and develop,
to gaze at sunsets,
and to look at the stars in wonder.
You think.
You perceive.
You follow the arc
of your marvelous, precious life,
all without the responsibility
of keeping it all afloat.
Miracles are cascading
upon us as we speak.
Raise your head and celebrate!

14

I take the bow of my mind
and pass it over the strings
of my mysterious being.
A lovely melody emerges
that is all me,
laced with the grandeur
of the Sublime.

15

How can I draw myself
closer to Being?
How can I open
to sense the Sublime?
How can I manage myself and my life
to get beyond space and time?
What must I do to expand myself
and escape from my flat little mind?
Give me directions.
Let's make a start.
Guide me and pull me
Into Your heart.

16

Sophistication is the enemy.
Simplicity is the friend.
We grow and we change
on our path through life,
pulled forward by
things we admire.
The basic things are better
to fill the hungers we feel.
Keep life simple
and keep it beautiful,
Watch closely to what you aspire.

17

The Cosmos is dancing
Its stately pavane
As I sit dreaming and musing.
It's not like a clock.
It's far greater than that.
It's more like a flower
that's blooming its way
to an unseen and unknown future day.
I sense Its subtle aliveness
in my cells and in my heart.
I feel Its intelligence surrounding me.
I've been caught in Its grip from the start.
It is radiating Itself into the world.
It is fueling my every thought.

18

I'm looking for the metaphor
that will capture my yearning heart.
I want to express my depths,
and my longing,
and the ineffable Presence I feel
just beneath the material world.
These forms are just the surface,
including me and all I love.
We are part of a Life
that is Cosmic in scope,
shimmering and sparkling,
unfolding and blossoming,
eternally turning Itself
into Its future shape.

19

Moment by moment
my life drips away.
I cannot halt its going.
I am on a conveyer belt
that is taking me to my death.
All I can do is wake up
and taste the ineffable One
that is beating my heart,
and pumping my lungs,
that is giving me every breath.

20

The well is deep.
The well is black.
There is Mystery where
I seek to reach.
I sit in my body
in my favorite chair,
and ponder how to get there.
I want to touch this Presence
that I feel in the space,
that I feel in my life,
that is hovering in the air.
But I seem to be trapped
in this body,
and I have no ready book
to instruct me and guide me
just how to do it,
or in which direction to look.

21

Loveliness is all around us,
waiting for our inspection.
The smell of rain on a pavement.
the exuberance of a Dahlia,
the trill of a bird
welcoming the sun
on a frosty, dewy morning.
It's all there on every occasion,
but we are lost in our separateness
and only half awake,
and we look right past it all.
We keep our heads down,
fixated on our problems,
trapped in our minds,
and destined to keep ourselves small.

22

We're moving toward the Formless Realm.
Life, not death, pervades it.
Unruffled, serene and silent,
It throws up the world around us,
then takes it back into Its heart.
We're brought here and held here
for just a while
to experience the world of forms.
Then, in due course,
we are sent and dissolved,
back into the Sea of Light,
the shimmering Sea of Livingness,
from which we were never apart.

23

Open your eyes to wonder.
See into the heart of things.
Life is foaming all around you.
A miracle is in each moment.
We are caught in a
dazzling Cosmic display
of fierce and patterned intelligence.
We can shake ourselves
awake and aware,
if we want to take the trouble.
We can open our eyes
to the great display,
and share in Its wondrous unfolding today.

24

I am patiently waiting
to develop myself,
to open my eyes,
to taste the wine.
It seems that I have waited for years.
While I lived my life
and walked the earth,
and laughed my laughs,
and feared my fears,
I was waiting
all that time
for the touch of the Divine.
I am still waiting.

25

Give me a moment of Your time.
Give me a taste of Your nectar.
Open my heart and touch me
with Your ineffable breath.
I long to lose my edges,
to burst through the limited me.
I know that will be,
simultaneously,
the end of the little me,
and the beginning of me
as the Cosmic Sea.

26

I cannot see why I'm here.
How do I matter
to the mysterious Wonder
that sparkles all around me?
I am living my modular life.
I was formed to do it, it seems.
But as I move through it
I'm reaching for more.
There must be more to it.
I can't see the core.
This must not be all I can be.
This must not be all I can see.
Though I'm struggling with limits,
and I'm small and inept,
truthfully,
I have the conviction,
from deep in my heart,
that somehow this Sea needs me.

27

This is the first moment
of the world.
Reality is ever-new.
Life is blooming and flaring
and metamorphosing Itself as we view.
The future is arriving.
It comes to us as today,
ever-fresh and startling
in Its own inimitable way.
It's never stale or in decay.
We are living in a flower
of miraculous, blossoming Life today.

28

A titan of industry
I could never be,
but if I was
could I possibly see
the heave and grace
of the Invisible One,
the vastness of beauty
beneath the world,
and in the world and
possibly,
possibly,
even in me?

29

I am a confluence of forces,
a host of rivulets merging,
and converging,
into the river I call my life.
I cannot see
what is forming me,
and taking me forward
into the day.
The people I talk to,
the words that I hear,
the decisions I make
to go here or there,
are a multitude of potentials,
inter-weaving themselves
as I watch,
beyond my control,
beyond my grasp,
the will of a master strategist
that puts my life together.

30

Have I been all that I could be?
Have I seen all that I could see?
I don't think so.
I think I know
I could have made more of me.
I went off on so many false starts.
I didn't have a plan.
I stumbled my way
from day to day,
confused and disoriented,
and continually spun all around.
This was hardly a map of success,
and yet,
as I look back in contemplation
over decades of turbulent life,
there are threads weaving
through the confusion.
There was something at the core.
It was messy but somehow coherent.
Something was trying to be.
As I floundered and flailed
through the passing years,
I was making the person
that I learned to call me.

31

The world is arising
from the mysterious depths
of living, unseen Power.
Invisible,
fecund,
and infinitely creative,
It stirs Itself
to create a Cosmos
and presents it to us,
Its latest creation.

32

Something is holding the world together.
Something is making it dance.
Deep patterns are arising now
to the surface of the world.
There is meaning here unfolding.
This is not the result of chance.
We arrive in a flurry of freshness,
we are dazzled by all that we see.
We try to see what is happening
but that is not to be.
We can only get glimpses of Glory
and Vastness,
and intimations of greater Life.
We are spun through our years
with our tears and our fears,
with no notion of how to see.

33

I know that I'm a primate,
with the animal soul on display.
I live in a bubble of self-concern,
pre-occupied with myself and today.
My mind is small
and I'm insecure.
I'm an ape walking on the earth,
but I'm growing and evolving,
and someday I'll be something new.
I will raise my head to the heavens
and the Cosmos will enter my view.
My mind will expand.
I will see myself
in the context of unfolding Life.
I will grow past this stage
of warfare and rage,
and become what I'm meant to be.

34

I'm surrounded by chimera.
Nothing is what it seems.
This solid world before my eyes
is the stuff that is made of dreams.
Each form is composed of galaxies,
ultra-small and whirling in place,
held together and looking concrete
but actually mostly space.
I look at the world in wonder.
It is not what it seems.
It is not where I live,
but I know I must grow
and be able to see
the chimera of material reality.

35

The Buddhists call it mindfulness,
to train your mind upon your mind
and rest it there, perceiving.
We live with a miracle behind our eyes,
a space of living sensitivity.
It makes our life possible.
It makes our life conscious.
It allows us to think and do,
and make our way through life.
We take it for granted.
We overlook.
We're lost in our thoughts.
We're half asleep,
but as long as we live
the gift is there,
sending and receiving,
registering and perceiving.
Grace is raining upon us.

36

This is the feeling
of being alive,
as I sit in my chair,
waiting for day.
I can feel the life
coursing through my limbs.
My mind is buzzing
in its usual way.
I'm receiving the gifts
of energy,
of consciousness,
of the trillion interactions per second
that keep me alive,
that keep me alert,
that keep me on earth in my chair,
ready and eager to go into life,
and ready to take Life's dare.

37

You cannot die into emptiness.
There's really nothing to fear.
The Cosmos around us is full,
not bare,
filled with particles coming and going.
We are living inside a Wholeness,
a single, vast living Mind.
There is nothing here
but Life,
Life,
Life,
and Its waiting for us
at the end of the line.

38

We are living in a rainbow world
though we don't perceive its colors.
Shifting,
flashing,
merging,
the colors meld together
to lace our reality.
We need to evolve to see this.
We need to grow new senses.
We need to expand our perceptions
to reach our destiny.

39

Something moves me through my day.
I can feel Its push,
I can feel Its pull.
I can feel that I have
a part to play,
never mind how small,
never mind how obscure.
I cannot see the pattern
of the vastness of the earth.
I cannot see
how the little me
fits into the astounding Whole.
I can only see that I'm here today,
breathing,
thinking,
being me,
part of a Splendor that has the power
to take my breath away.

40

I want to dig deeper into myself.
I know there's Divinity here,
but it's covered by layers
of human concerns,
and lost in the welter
of living life.
If I'm silent and still
perhaps I can see
beneath the superficial me
to the core of myself
as the Cosmos,
shining brilliantly.

41

If I was the only person on Earth,
and no-one was there to applaud,
would I live the way
I am living today?
Would I fill my mind
with the urge to be seen?
I don't think so.
Perhaps with no-one around,
I could finally be free
of the impulse to play to the bleachers.
I know that my real relationship
is with the vast Unseen.
I'm a part of the Cosmic unfolding.
This is where my value lies.
I don't really need to be noticed.
It's a siren singing a false song.
But I seem to be trapped
by the longing
for attention and approval of my peers.
Just keep growing.
Just keep maturing.
Just keep stretching yourself.
It's a problem that likely could take
every one of your remaining years.

42

I want to put myself in contact
with the Cosmic Presence
that is in this room,
that is in the world,
that is throwing up all that I see.
But how do I do that right now?
Give me a way to touch You.
Open Your arms to me.
Fill up my heart with
Your brimming Life.
Enter my surging cells.
I want to feel Your intimacy.
Come share Yourself now with me.

43

Do you believe in destiny,
that we were brought here
for a reason?
Do you believe that you chose
your entry point and more?
Do you believe that you're learning
what your soul must learn to grow,
that you're pushed from
lesson to lesson
to learn what your soul must know?
We're pummeled and pushed
through a turbulent life.
We're spun all around and dazzled.
We can't understand
even though we try.
It leaves us disheveled and frazzled.
But beneath the turmoil and pain
there is order here unfolding.
We are coming to know ourselves.
We are coming to know the Cosmos.
This is a school for souls.

44

I'm trying to grow myself bigger.
I'm trying to see deeper
than I could before.
An impulse is pressing inside me
to examine and explore,
and to strongly reach for,
the intangible Presence of Spirit,
the unfolding life of the Cosmos,
the emerging will of Being,
all this, and much, much more.
This search is not just mine.
I feel it is fueled by Something divine.
I'm in the grip of Power here
that is seeking to express Itself.
If It comes through me,
I'm delighted to be
the instrument of Its expression.

45

The earth spins effortlessly,
perfectly held in its place
in space,
and dancing with the Sun.
My heart beats effortlessly,
beyond my will,
beyond my mind.
It will beat until
my sojourn here is over.
We are caught in
a web of Power
that is spinning the earth,
that is beating our hearts,
that is causing the Cosmos to be.
Open your eyes.
Open your heart.
There are miracles here to see.

46

I wait for the touch
of Your radiance.
I long for Your ecstasy too.
I am nothing without Your power.
My resources are too few.
I'm in the position of suppliant here.
I can't do it on my own.
I want to be close
to Your beating heart.
I want the gifts
of Your miraculous Whole.
Come near me now
and open my heart,
and pour Yourself into my soul.

47

I bow my head.
I open my heart.
I still my mind,
and I wait.
I do all the things
that I know to do
to expand myself,
to prepare myself,
and I wait.
But in this moment
I can see
that it is not to be.
Your Presence,
it is clear right now,
is not entirely up to me.

48

We cannot understand our life,
no matter how we try.
We don't have the right equipment
to see deeply,
and truly,
into the heart of things.
We are driven by longing
to take our place
in this shimmering Cosmos
of Living Space,
but it's elusive and mysterious
and often too remote to touch.
We can get just a glimpse
of Something sublime,
but our world is grey
too much of the time.

49

Open my eyes
and open my heart,
and let me truly see
the miraculous Cosmos
we are swimming in,
the miracle it is to be.

50

How should we hold them in our heart,
those who are dear to us?
How close should we be
when we can see
that they live in fragility?
What risk should we take in loving them?
What pain should we dare
to share?
It takes courage to love
when we are aware
that every love ends in tragedy.

51

There's more to me
than I can see.
There are many layers here.
I go through my day
on the surface of things,
on the surface of me,
though I may be
yearning for depth every minute.
In moments of contemplation
I see beyond my mind,
with its chaos and chatter
and self-concern
and superficiality.
In those moments I sense a radiance
that is blooming there inside.
There is Something watching,
and waiting,
and nudging,
and guiding,
and leading me
to be what I am destined to be,
to see what I am destined to see.

52

We are a moving stream
of possibilities,
evolving,
unfolding,
emerging on the earth,
and slowly,
slowly,
and painfully,
becoming what we will be.

53

Apes on the earth,
murderous,
what can you expect?
We are not yet finished becoming.
We are growing out of our past.
We are emerging,
slowly and painfully,
from the earth itself,
not yet a high life-form,
not yet finished and polished
into a beautiful thing.
We are now in an in-between place
with one foot in the celestial
and the other in the bestial.
Now we have poems to write,
so to grow,
Now we have songs to sing.

54

We might yet be saved
from ourselves.
We might yet be given a way.
We might yet be turned aside
from the murderous path
that we are on today.
The Cosmos is ever-resourceful.
We cannot predict Its response.
We must do our part,
and lie in wait
for opportunity to appear.
But it's not just up to us.
There is more here than we can see.
If we're to be saved
from the path we are on,
and allowed to continue our experiment,
we'll need to call upon the creativity
of the marvelous Cosmic Sea.

55

So many memories.
So much life.
My mind reaches back
across the decades.
All those people
I loved and knew,
all gone,
all disappeared.
We don't realize,
as we live our life,
that it is vanishing
right behind us.
Wake up!
Attend to the sweetness.
It will be gone in a minute.

56

How should we view
this world of today?
Should we be lost in despair?
It seems to be erupting—
with violence,
and greed,
and destruction.
Is there a way forward
that is not filled with death?
Perhaps we can change our perspective.
Perhaps this is only a surface storm,
a tempest above the Ocean of Life.
Drop into the depths of Being,
to the bottom of the Sea.
There is no storm raging
down there in the depths.
It is silent and still.
It is eternity.

57

If I could go deeper
perhaps I could see
the astonishing rainbow
surrounding me.
The marvelous spectacle
that is the earth,
bursting and blooming
with colored light.
I know it is there
but I cannot see.
It is veiled by familiarity.

58

My subject is eternity.
My canvas is the Cosmos.
I look and I find vast riches
pouring upon my head.
I'm the creation of Creation.
I'm a miracle walking here.
I can dance with the Life-Force evolving
if I can just wake up
and move beyond my fear.

59

I know that You are everywhere.
I know that You are everything.
There is no space
where You are not.
You lie in every direction.
I live my life in Your marvelous Field.
You beat my heart.
You pump my lungs.
You fire my little mind.
I know that when my wounds appear,
In You they can be healed.

60

How do I align myself
with the Field of Living Space?
How do I get closer
to the Source of Life,
the Source of Miracle?
What do I do to open up
to Reality Supreme?
What is the way
I can deepen myself,
and stretch myself,
and expand myself
to touch the Vast Unseen?

61

Waiting for understanding.
Reaching for meaning.
Yearning for depth.
Longing
for belonging.
I am a study in unfilled appetites.
I am basically incomplete.
I feel my incompleteness intensely,
and I am driven to try to fill my holes.
In moments Something arrives
and I move beyond this state.
The next moment, however,
I am back again,
grasping at the world,
grasping at other people,
grasping at the Cosmos,
trying to create a something
out of myself,
trying to relieve the empty nothing
that I feel at the center of my heart.

62

Make a comrade of loss.
When life hands you
sudden and unexpected desolation,
and after you have vented
your astonishment,
and regrets,
and rage
at the injustice of it all,
try to cozy up to loss.
Let it in your door.
Give it a place at your table.
Accept it as,
if not a friend,
a familiar and tiresome companion.
In time its effects will diminish.
Life will resume.
Pain will lessen,
and you will go forward
with your wound that,
though it will never vanish away,
will stop its bleeding for now.

63

Who is in charge here
of my becoming?
Who is driving this train?
I always thought it was me.
Lately, however, I begin to see
that there is more going on here
than I knew.
I see patterns emerging,
and effects arising,
and learning appearing
from that which I did not choose.
I am growing in ways
that I could not foresee,
in the grip of an Intelligence,
and in the pulsing of a Cosmic dance,
that is greater than,
and evolving of,
this minuscule, self-absorbed me.

64

Morning arrives with its radiance.
The world is again made anew.
Fresh prospects arise
and present themselves,
borne in with the morning dew.
My aging heart is quickened.
My hopes somehow resurrect.
The future looks brighter to me.
My fears disappear from view.
I'm filled with the possibilities
of burgeoning, surging Life
arising now in the morning,
from the Cosmic well
of the bottomless New.

65

What if we are not the doer?
What if it's all a game?
What if our clawing at the world
is not required or sane?
What if we are moving through
the arc of our life
as a piece in a master plan
that is vaster than we can imagine,
that is grander than we can conceive.
What if we raised our heads to the sky
and found something
that we could truly believe?

66

If I clear my mind
and I wait,
Something will move
through my soul.
If I can stop thinking of me,
Something arises that I can see
is vaster than anything
I could be.
So this is the game.
This is the plan.
This is to be my fate.
I will clear my mind.
I will open myself,
and I will
wait,
wait,
wait.

67

It's a great gift to be human,
to have,
at your disposal,
a mind that was forged over eons,
and partakes of the
Conscious Cosmos.
Have you thought of this?
Have you considered
the meticulous care
that was lavished upon the making
of the awareness that you call you?

68

I bow to the moon,
circling our earth and watching
the cavalcade of our making.
How many triumphs has it seen?
How many massacres,
and betrayals,
and acts of heroism,
and fabulous breakthroughs,
and acts of selflessness
in the slowly unfolding
arc of our narrative,
as we grow from the beasts
to the angels.

69

What are we becoming?
Where are we going
with this uncontrollable,
burgeoning,
chaotic development
that is propelling us
into an unknown and uncertain future,
without plan or design.
I hope the Cosmos is caring for us,
and fashioning our progress forward,
because we are certainly not.

70

Somewhere galaxies are colliding.
Somewhere a star explodes.
Somewhere the heart of the Cosmos
is fashioning a world to be.
As we walk on the earth
with our heads down,
lost in our little ambitions,
pre-occupied, separate and self-concerned,
we are missing the miracles
that are here to see.

71

Under the clamor of the world
a vast and silent peace exists.
The sound
around
us on the earth
arises from this place.
Material forms too
that we can view
all around us in our life
are arising now from Nothingness
thrown up by Living Space.

72

Creativity is a flow.
The fresh and the new
come into view
from a Source
that is deep and hidden.
We can step into Its river.
We can partake of Its grace.
We can share
in the burgeoning newness
thrown up by
living, creative Space.

73

We march side by side with others.
We may think they belong to us.
We fail to see,
through familiarity,
that they are a universe of their own.
There are billions of us on the earth now,
marching along together,
each perfectly unique,
an experiment in form,
and evolution,
and meaning.
Together we are coalescing,
living our way,
slowly,
slowly,
into the future that we will be.

74

When you're nearing the end of the road
everything seems to light up.
Everything becomes more unique, more precious.
You begin to see through the veils
of familiarity,
and conditioning,
and every-dayness,
to the beauty of the usual,
and the sweetness of Life
blazing in the world around,
and blazing in those that you love.

75

Can you grasp how precious your life is?
Can you,
for one moment,
rise above the obsession
with your little problems and crises,
and let your mind burst free,
to roam in the stars
and flare with the suns,
and turn with the earth,
eternally?

76

Something that is greater than me
is writing this poem as I watch.
Something is rising from the depths.
As It beats my heart,
as It makes my day,
It is making this poem
in Its artless way.
It is using me
and coming through me
because It has something
It wants to say.
I must get out of Its way.

77

You cannot be overlooked.
There cannot be,
in this vast, vast Sea,
a hidden part that goes unseen.
Every part of the Cosmos
is a part of the Whole.
Every thought that you think
goes throughout.
You cannot be disconnected.
There is no separate locality.
You are living your life
in the arms
of Consciousness,
of Mystery,
of Livingness.
You are kept here
by Vastness and Beauty.
Relax and open your eyes.
There's a living rainbow touching the earth
and it fills the Cosmic skies.